Easy Concert Pieces
Leichte Konzertstücke

for Piano
für Klavier

Volume 3 / Band 3:
41 Easy Pieces from 4 Centuries
41 leichte Stücke aus 4 Jahrhunderten

Grade / Schwierigkeitsgrad:
easy to intermediate / leicht bis mittelschwer

Edited by / Herausgegeben von
Rainer Mohrs and / und Monika Twelsiek

CD Recording / CD-Einspielung:
Vera Sacharowa

ED 22549
ISMN 979-0-001-16132-9
ISBN 978-3-7957-1059-0

Volume 1 / Band 1:
sehr leicht / very easy
ED 22547

Volume 2 / Band 2:
leicht / easy
ED 22548

www.schott-music.com

Mainz · London · Berlin · Madrid · New York · Paris · Prague · Tokyo · Toronto
© 2017 SCHOTT MUSIC GmbH & Co. KG, Mainz · Printed in Germany

Preface

The 'Easy Concert Pieces' series presents easy piano pieces in progressive order. These pieces are intended to complement a piano tutorial method and are particularly suitable for performance at auditions, concerts, competitions and examinations. They offer varied repertoire in a broad selection of pieces from the Baroque, Classical, Romantic and Modern eras.

Volume 1 contains pieces in the five-note range and easy pieces spanning a single octave. Other criteria for selection are simple rhythms and very easy chords. Crossing the thumb underneath, playing several parts together and pedalling are not yet required.

Volume 2 contains pieces with an extended range of two octaves. Crossing the thumb under, pedal use, simple polyphony and three- or four-part chords all feature here, as do simple ornaments, playing cantabile and differentiating between melody and accompaniment.

Volume 3 is intended for advanced players who wish to work on expressive playing and individual interpretation. These pieces demand greater fluency and rhythmic control, more advanced articulation and phrasing, polyphonic harmonies (playing several parts even with one hand) and differentiation of tone and touch.

Vorwort

Die Reihe „Easy Concert Pieces" enthält leichte Klavierstücke in progressiver Reihenfolge. Die Stücke sind als Ergänzung zur Klavierschule gedacht und eignen sich besonders für das Vorspiel an Musikschulen, für Wettbewerbe und für Prüfungen. Die Repertoireauswahl ist vielseitig und bietet eine vielfältige Auswahl an Stücken aus Barock, Klassik, Romantik und Moderne.

Band 1 enthält Stücke im Fünftonraum und leichte Stücke im einfachen Oktavraum. Weitere Kriterien für die Auswahl waren einfache Rhythmik und sehr leichtes Akkordspiel. Daumenuntersatz, polyphone Mehrstimmigkeit und Pedalspiel werden noch nicht vorausgesetzt.

Band 2 enthält Stücke im erweiterten Tonumfang von 2 Oktaven. Vorausgesetzt werden Daumenuntersatz, Pedalspiel, einfache Polyphonie und drei- bis vierstimmiges Akkordspiel, einfache Verzierungen, cantables Spiel und Differenzierung zwischen Melodie und Begleitung.

Band 3 wendet sich an fortgeschrittene Spieler, die an ausdrucksvollem Spiel und eigenständiger Interpretation arbeiten wollen. Die Stücke stellen höhere Ansprüche an Geläufigkeit und Rhythmik, Artikulation und Phrasierung, polyphones Spiel (Mehrstimmigkeit auch in einer Hand) und an die klangliche Differenzierung des Klaviersatzes.

Rainer Mohrs / Monika Twelsiek
English Translation Julia Rushworth

CD Recording / CD-Einspielung: Vera Sacharowa
Aufnahme: Studio Tonmeister, Mainz
Die Klavierstücke Nr. 9, 10, 17 spielt Wilhelm Ohmen
Die Klavierstücke Nr. 6, 14, 25, 27 spielt Karin Germer
© 2017 Schott Music GmbH & Co. KG, Mainz
Printed in Germany · BSS 57577

Contents / Inhalt

Chaconne

D Minor / d-Moll / Ré mineur
HWV 448

Georg Friedrich Händel
1685–1759

Praeludium

F major / F-Dur / Fa majeur

BWV 927

Johann Sebastian Bach
1685–1750

from /aus: J. S. Bach, 12 little Preludes / 12 kleine Präludien, Schott ED 0849

Praeludium

D minor / d-Moll

BWV 926

Johann Sebastian Bach

from /aus: J. S. Bach, 12 little Preludes / 12 kleine Präludien, Schott ED 0849

Inventio 1
C major / C-Dur
BWV 772

Johann Sebastian Bach

from / aus: J. S. Bach, 15 Two Part Inventions / 15 zweistimmige Inventionen, Schott ED 01092

Inventio 4

D minor / d-Moll

BWV 775

Johann Sebastian Bach

from / aus: J. S. Bach, 15 Two Part Inventions / 15 zweistimmige Inventionen, Schott ED 01092

a)

(~ ad lib.)

b) (𝄢 ad lib.)

Rondeau
D major / D-Dur
KV 15d

Wolfgang Amadeus Mozart
1756 – 1791

Fine

D. C. al Fine

from / aus: The young Mozart / Der junge Mozart, Schott 9008

Bagatelle
A minor / a-Moll
op. 119/9

Ludwig van Beethoven
1770–1827

Vivace assai ed un poco sentimentale *)

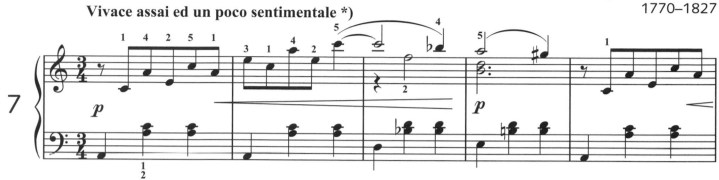

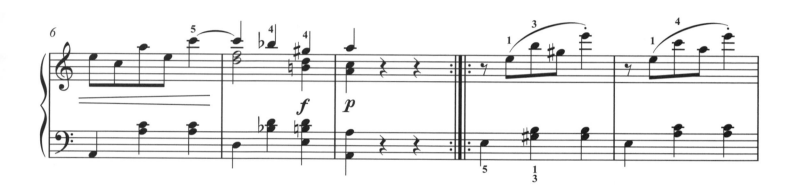

*) According to the autograph / Nach dem Autograph

Für Elise

WoO 59

Ludwig van Beethoven

*) First Edition / Erstausgabe (1867): e only in bar 7 / nur in Takt 7. Beethoven's autograph sketch / autograph Skizze: d

Sonatine

F major / F-Dur

Ludwig van Beethoven

Allegro assai ♩ = 96

Rondo

Sonatina / Sonatine
C major / C-Dur
I

Tobias Haslinger
1787–1842

Allegro non tanto

II

Tobias Haslinger

Allegretto

Waltz / Walzer

B minor / h-Moll
op. 18/6

Franz Schubert
1797–1828

Arabesque

Frédéric Burgmüller
1806–1874

Allegro scherzando (♩ = 132)

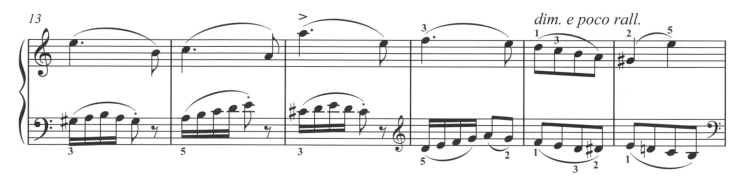

from / aus: F. Burgmüller, 25 easy Studies / 25 leichte Etüden, op. 100, Schott ED 173

Ballad / Ballade

Frédéric Burgmüller

from / aus: F. Burgmüller, 25 easy Studies / 25 leichte Etüden, op. 100, Schott ED 173

Romance
Romanze

Felix Mendelssohn-Bartholdy
1809–1847

Wild Horseman / Wilder Reiter

op. 68/8

Robert Schumann
1810–1856

from / aus: R. Schumann, Album for the Young / Album für die Jugend, Schott ED 9010

Siciliana / Sizilianisch
op. 68/11

Robert Schumann

Schalkhaft ♩. = 116

18

cresc.

♩ = 100

Schluss / Fine

Vom Anfang ohne Wiederholungen bis zum Schluss
D. C. al Fine senza ripetizione

from / aus: R. Schumann, Album for the Young / Album für die Jugend, Schott ED 9010

First Loss / Erster Verlust

op. 68/16

Robert Schumann

Nicht schnell ♩ = 56 – 63

Etwas langsamer

Im

Tempo

from / aus: R. Schumann, Album for the Young / Album für die Jugend, Schott ED 9010

Waltz / Walzer
A minor / a-Moll
op. posth.

Frédéric Chopin
1810–1849

Polonaise
G minor / g-Moll

Frédéric Chopin

Erstausgabe (1817) ohne Dynamik und Bögen / First edition (1817) without dynamics and phrasing

Polonaise D. C. al Fine

Mazurka
G minor / g-Moll
opus 67 No. 2

Frédéric Chopin

from / aus: F. Chopin, 20 selected Mazurkas / 20 ausgewählte Mazurken, Schott ED 9022

Mazurka

F major / F-Dur

op. 68/3

Frédéric Chopin

Allegro, ma non troppo ♩ = 120

Study

Etüde
op. 45/2

Stephen Heller
1814–1888

Allegro vivace ♩ = 160

from / aus: S. Heller, 25 melodious Studies / 25 melodische Etüden op. 45

Sweet Dreaming

Süße Träumerei

op. 39/21

Peter Iljitsch Tschaikowsky
1840–1893

Waltz
Walzer

op. 12/2

Edvard Grieg
1843–1907

Allegro moderato ♩. = 60

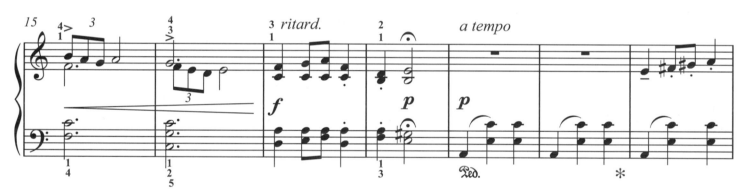

from / aus: Lyric Pieces / Lyrische Stücke, Schott ED 9011

27 CD

Le petit nègre

Cakewalk

Claude Debussy
1862–1918

Allegro giusto ♩ = 108 – 116

Gymnopédie No. 1

Erik Satie
1866–1925

D. C. al ⊕ – ⊕

Gnossienne No. 2

Erik Satie

Siciliana
(1920)

Allegretto dolcemente mosso ♩. = ca. 52

Alfredo Casella
1883–1947

(il ritmo sempre molto preciso)

Tango I
(1933)

Mátyás Seiber
1905–1960

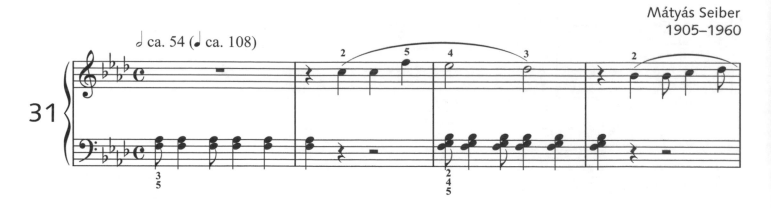

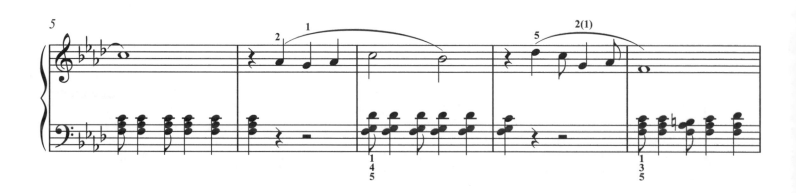

from / aus: M. Seiber, Easy Dances / Leichte Tänze, Schott ED 2234

Tango II
(Habanera)

Mátyás Seiber

from / aus: M. Seiber, Easy Dances / Leichte Tänze, Schott ED 2234

Blue Waltz
(1976)

Eduard Pütz
1911–2000

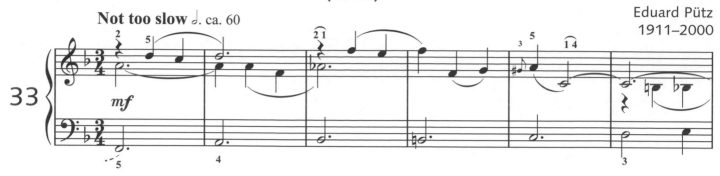

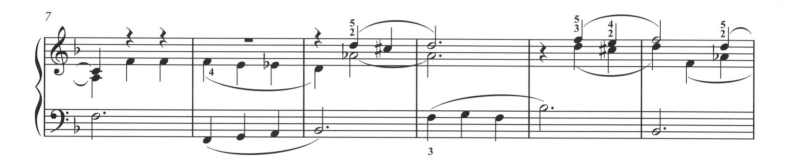

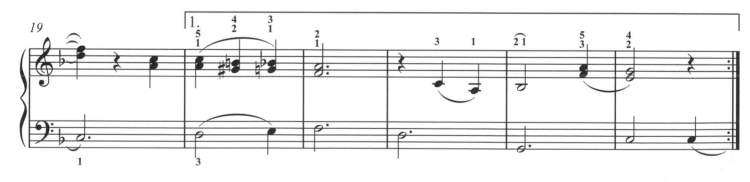

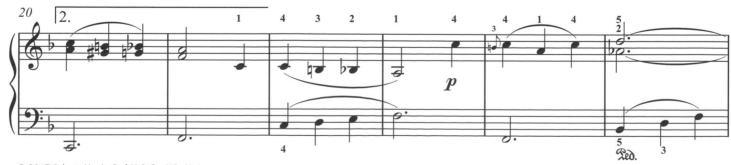

from / aus: E. Pütz, Mr. Clementi goin' on holidays, Schott ED 6662

Homecoming / Heimkehr

op. 118/1

Harald Weiss
* 1949

from / aus: H. Weiss, My blue diary / Mein blaues Tagebuch, Schott ED 8288

Jumping Dance / Springtanz
op. 118/2

Harald Weiss

Lightly moving, Trot / Leicht bewegt, Trab (♩ = 88)

from / aus: H. Weiss, My blue diary / Mein blaues Tagebuch, Schott ED 8288

Prayer for Peace

Rainer Mohrs
*1953

Melancholy Reflections

Mike Schoenmehl
* 1957

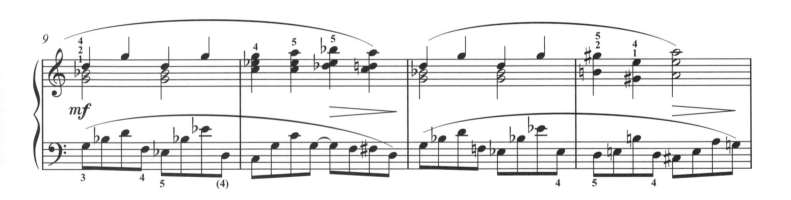

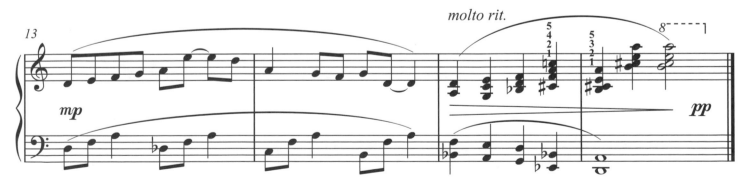

from / aus: M. Schoenmehl, Piano Studies in Pop, Schott ED 7304

The Sunken Island of Atlantis
Die versunkene Insel Atlantis

Hans-Günter Heumann
*1955

from / aus: H.-G. Heumann, Fantasy Piano, 20 Enchanting Easy Piano Pieces / 20 zauberhafte Klavierstücke, Schott ED 22111

39 CD

Hallo Kätzchen!

Hallo Kitty!

Vera Mohrs
*1984

Timmy is so happy: he has been given a kitten for his birthday! At first the shy creature hides behind the curtain, peeping out inquisitively. Soon it is strokking its fur around Timmy's legs, purring happily.

Timmy ist überglücklich: Zum Geburtstag hat er ein Kätzchen bekommen! Zuerst versteckt sich das schüchterne Tier hinter der Gardine und lugt neugierig hervor. Aber schon bald streicht es um Timmys Beine und schnurrt freundlich.

from / aus: V. Mohrs, Cat Songs / Katzenmusik, 12 Little Piano Stories / 12 kleine Klaviergeschichten, Schott ED 20372

Poor Mouse

Arme Maus

Vera Mohrs

A little mouse is gnawing at a biscuit in the larder.
The cat creeps up stealthily and puts its claws out.
What happens next?

In der Vorratskammer ist ein Mäuschen und knabbert an
einem Keks. Die Katze schleicht sich vorsichtig an und
fährt ihre Krallen aus. Was passiert dann?

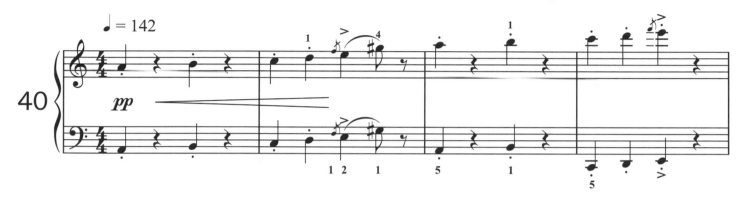

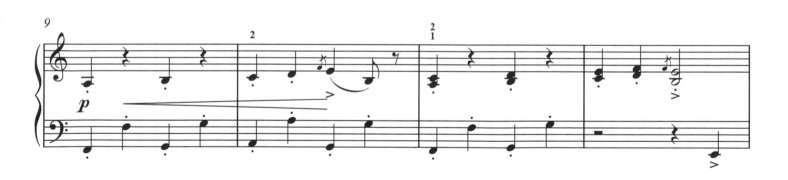

from / aus: V. Mohrs, Cat Songs / Katzenmusik, 12 Little Piano Stories / 12 kleine Klaviergeschichten, Schott ED 20372

41 CD

Cats in Love

Verliebte Katzen

Shyly the kitten approaches the unfamiliar ginger tom sitting outside at the edge of the road. She miaows hesitantly and brushes along the garden fence, purring, until at last the tomcat leaps across towards her!

Schüchtern nähert sich das Kätzchen dem fremden Kater, der jetzt draußen am Straßenrand sitzt. Sie miaut zaghaft und streicht schnurrend am Gartenzaun entlang, bis der Kater endlich zu ihr herüberspringt!

Vera Mohrs

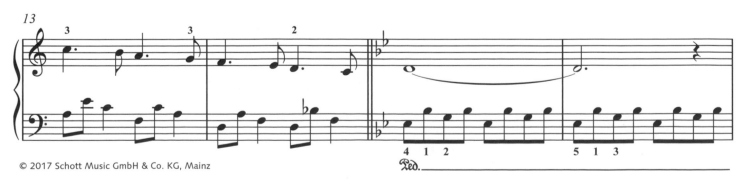

from / aus: V. Mohrs, Cat Songs / Katzenmusik, 12 Little Piano Stories / 12 kleine Klaviergeschichten, Schott ED 20372

Schott Music, Mainz 57577